PSALMS
in the
KEY *of* LIFE

PSALMS
in the
KEY *of* LIFE

David L. Dollison, Sr.

XULON PRESS

Xulon Press
2301 Lucien Way #415
Maitland, FL 32751
407.339.4217
www.xulonpress.com

© 2021 by David L. Dollison, Sr.

All rights reserved solely by the author. The author guarantees all contents are original and do not infringe upon the legal rights of any other person or work. No part of this book may be reproduced in any form without the permission of the author. The views expressed in this book are not necessarily those of the publisher.

Unless otherwise indicated, Scripture quotations taken from the King James Version (KJV) – *public domain*.

Printed in the United States of America.

Paperback ISBN-13: 978-1-6628-1073-2
Ebook ISBN-13: 978-1-6628-1074-9

Thank you and Dedications

First, I would like to thank God for blessing me with encouraging words and people throughout my lifetime.

Even though she is no longer with us, I would like to thank my mother-in-law, Vera Mae Johnson, for being my sounding board and for her words of encouragement.

I would like to thank my five children, Deonca, Danielle, Demanesse, David Jr., and Desmond for pushing me to write my story.

I would like to thank my former church family, Faith Presbyterian Church, which encouraged me to write poems for church events.

I also want to thank Pastor Michael Jones, Sr. for his constant encouragement.

To my niece Charity Byrd for typing the extremely rough

draft of the manuscript. Thank you for making sense of my scribbles.

While I can't remember all of those who encouraged me, you know who you are, and I would like to thank you for believing in me.

Last, but not least, to my wife of fifty-one years, Phyl—thank you for being my tough-love editor throughout the years.

Table of Contents

Foreword ix
Beginnings 1
General Overview of Life Growing Up 5
Life in Chicago 13
Back to Muncie 17
Married Life 25
Military Life 27
Back to Civilian Life 37
Last Thoughts and Ending Prayers 45
Writing Poetry 51
    Mother's Day 53
    Memorial Day 54
    In Time 55
    Tribute to Dr. King 57
    Chosen 60
    Where's My Man? 62

Psalms in the Key of Life

33 Years 64
Secrets 65
A Good Man 66
Legacy 68
The Making of a Black Man 70
Care to Love 71
Chains 73
Happy 55th 75
To Marcus, My Son 77
Mama's Girl 80
Be Young, Be Foolish, Be Happy 81
A Celebration of Life –
    Dr. Reverend Frank Jackson 83
Grandson 85
Jason 87
Mona 88
Thanksgiving 89
This House 91
A Tribute to Ms. Vivian Dickens 92
Homegoing 94

Foreword

As you read this book, undoubtedly, you will not agree with some or all of it. However, there is one thing you must keep in mind. This story takes place in a simpler time—in a time when a man's handshake meant something. When in most places, people watched out for their neighbors. If someone saw trouble, he or she would lend a hand in some way instead of what often happens today, which is watching for enjoyment or worse, taking pictures to see if the picture will go viral on social media. (For those who take pictures/videos to hold others accountable or to stop bad behavior, thank you).

It was a time when children played outside (games such as tag, tether ball, ring-around-the-rosey, Mother May I?, etc.). Young people actually talked to each other instead of being glued to video games or social media. It was a time when people had and were taught morals, modesty, and decency, a time when children knew and respected their boundaries and understood that stepping outside of the boundaries meant a spanking. (**Side Note 1:** I'll stop right here for a moment for those hollering, "That's child abuse!" There are several scriptures in the Bible that teach how to raise a child, and one that comes readily to mind is, "If you spare the rod, you spoil the child," so, yes, spanking is okay. It takes good judgement, compassion, and a lot of consideration, but children must have and know their boundaries. Some children may respond better to other forms of discipline, but that should be up to the parents, not the government.)

It was a time when a lie was a lie, not matter how it was described, presented, or twisted, and the truth was the truth. You get the point…it was different time with, thankfully, different rules.

I would like to invite you to take a journey with me through a few of the chronicles in my life. This journey is of how a young black boy, teen, and man dealt with some of his life experiences. My hope is that it will help you with some the challenges you may be facing at this time in your life. The problems may be different, but the challenges I faced are just as relevant as the ones you may be dealing with today.

Beginnings

My maternal grandfather was Smith Thompson, and he was born in Huntsville, Alabama. My maternal grandmother, Lucille Benefield, was also born in Huntsville, Alabama. They met and married in Huntsville and lived there before they moved to Chattanooga, Tennessee, before eventually moving to Muncie, Indiana.

Grandpa Thompson was able to purchase a house in Muncie in the early twenties, which in that time was a huge achievement for a black man. Grandpa and Grandma Thompson and their six children lived in the house for a number of years. My mom was born in 1921, the youngest of seven children. Mom's mother, Lucille, died when she was very young, and Grandfather later remarried Mama Sally.

Fast forward approximately thirty years to me—my name is David Lee Dollison, Sr., and I was born in Muncie, Indiana. By the time I was born, Grandpa's house was older and needed many repairs, but it belonged to us. We didn't have to pay rent, and it kept us dry and out of the elements. We had indoor plumbing, and we even had an indoor toilet (back in those days, some homes still had an outdoor privy). For heating, we had a warm-morning potbellied stove in the living room and a smaller four-burner stove in the kitchen that Mom cooked meals on.

My earliest memories were of my grandfather, Mama Sally, my parents, my four brothers, and I living in a two-bedroom, one-bath house with a small bunk area in the back. There were three generations in one house -- it was crowded, but it worked, and we all thrived.

When I was around five, I remember Grandpa getting up early and fixing a pot of coffee, and he would give me some in a cup of my own. My mother wasn't happy with this, but it was my first taste of the beverage. Regrettably, my grandfather died when I was six or seven. After Grandpa's death, we continued to live with Mama Sally until we moved to Chicago. Before I go into my years in Chicago, I believe a general overview of my younger years is in order.

General Overview of Life Growing Up

As written previously, I had a very humble start in life, and by the time I was born, our family was very poor. We were so poor that we could only lay claim to "po!" The "or" came as we reached our late teens and the oldest would leave home. Often, there was little food in the house that held Mama Sally, our parents, and five growing boys. Assistance for poor families during that time consisted of what was called commodities: butter, cheese, powdered milk, eggs, oatmeal, and some type of canned meat, which was distributed once a month. As far as I know, at that time, there was no monetary public assistance.

When times were really lean, we had a wagon that we would take down to the railroad tracks and pick up coal or damaged railroad ties that we could fit in our wagon. Our gleanings were taken back to the house, where we chopped the ties and then stacked them so Mom or Dad could put them in either stove. In the winter months, we shoveled snow off the porches and walkways of our house as well as the neighbors'. Our other chores included cleaning the house and washing our clothes (at the time, we didn't have a washing machine; we had a tub and a scrubbing board).

When my mother was ill, I became the cook for the family, in addition to all my other chores. Besides doing our chores, we had to make sure our homework was done and that we got to school on time. While we were at school, good behavior was expected. Anything less would receive a spanking. When it was report card time, A's and B's were good, C's would get you lectured, and D's or F's were not accepted and constituted a "parent consultation," i.e., a spanking.

Most of the clothes that I had came from the Salvation Army, and a lot of my pants had more patches on them than actual original material. My shoes were

Buster Brown brogans, and if we couldn't afford to get newer shoes, we would cut a cardboard print of our feet and place it in the shoes to keep our feet off of the ground as much as possible. Back in those days, gym class was a requirement, and I had a pair of P.F. Flyers for gym.

Even though mom and dad had little formal education—Mom had an eighth-grade education, and Dad had a sixth-grade education, they both preached about the importance of education in our lives. It wasn't until years later that I understood why they had been insistent about it.

(**Side Note 2.** In school, especially high school, although my parents didn't know it, I was told constantly that I was only qualified to do the most menial jobs, and my curriculum was chosen by counselors who didn't have my best interest at heart. This changed when Phyl and I got married and she went to back to school. My counselor mistakenly called her to the office (because she had my last name) and tried to run the same game on her. Phyl wasn't having it. She had been brought up in a more advanced school system with advanced classes, and she knew what she was capable of. She realized how I had been counseled and she became angry on my behalf. She would tell me to forget them what I had been told all my life and that I was extremely intelligent and could do whatever I wanted to do. I believed her.)

(**Side Note 3.** Most of my schooling was in Muncie, and most of the school system was used to hold back black children, gearing them toward lower-paying jobs (laborer, housekeeper, etc.). Unless your family had some influence or money, you, in the school system's mind, were a servant, and you were educated as such.)

In our house, respecting our parents and adults was taught and expected. You were going to respect Mom and Dad and obey the rules of the house, and, most importantly, you knew not to do anything that would bring the police to the house because of something you had done.

You learned the hierarchy of life. First God, then Mom and Dad, then all adults, and then you. When I was young, any adult had authority over you, and you knew to respect them. You were taught to say, "Yes, sir" and "Yes, ma'am." If you were doing anything wrong, other adults in the community had permission to spank you. You were then sent home, where you got another spanking for embarrassing your parents by your actions. For those brought up in the fifties and sixties, "It takes a whole village to raise a child," had deep meaning, and you didn't dare question it.

These rules seem to have all but fallen away from today's society. The pendulum has swung too far the other way, where the parent(s) are subject to the will of the child. If you discipline your child like I was during the 1960s, you will end up in jail. With very little or no boundaries, children (people) have spiraled out of control. When lawbreaking happens (real, imaged, or otherwise), the police have the authority to stop, shoot, and kill your child (if you're a minority, at least).

(**Side Note 4.** In light of the many police killings of black and brown people today, I will say this. There are two sides of justice to the American dream. On my side of the American dream, the excessive and brutal behavior of the police is almost always justified. When the police are sued and found to be wrong, they settle for a sum of money with a gag order, which prevents the victim from talking about the incident ever again. What kind of justice do we have when those who are supposed to protect and serve the community instead act as judge, jury, and executioner and kill people instead? To add insult to injury, our tax dollars are used to pay for their crimes. They still walk around free, and in some cases, they go on to kill others. On the other side of the American dream is white privilege. The only thing I can tell you about that side is that the benefit of the doubt in all things appears to be the norm, not the automatic assumption of guilt.)

I believe a small prayer is in order: Dear God, I thank you for watching over me and blessing me with the life I've had. I thank you for helping me avoid life's traps and snares that come with living in an unequal society, that I can be an encourager for those younger brothers and sisters who come along after me and let them know that the old saying, "Life is hard, but it's

General Overview of Life Growing Up

fair," didn't always apply because of the color of my skin. Help me to show them that even though life may be hard, if they cling to You, they will have greater joy in life and less despair. Help me to tell them that they can pass on hope and encouragement to their children and grandchildren as well.

LIFE IN CHICAGO

SHORTLY AFTER GRANDPA'S DEATH, WE MOVED to Chicago. Dad worked at Campbell Soup, and before we moved, he would come home on the weekends (money permitting). It was the late 1950s when we moved to the South Side of Chicago. I remember several things about Chicago—one, the extremely cold winters; two, the gangs; and three, the trouble I got into at school.

Chicago weather was and is extremely cold. I gained first-hand knowledge of why it's dubbed "the Windy City." It was common for the temperature in the winter months to be -10 to -30 degrees with the wind chill factor. Your whole body had to be covered adequately in order to avoid getting frostbite. Thankfully, we had the winter clothes we needed to stay warm.

Psalms in the Key of Life

Going to school, I remember my older brother getting into trouble often and that my parents had to go to his school several times. My older brother's bad example helped me to learn how to stay out of trouble. I was determined to be good at school. There were a few blimps, but I was determined. Unfortunately, I reckoned this without thinking of the gangs and the bullies.

Even back in the late fifties, there were gangs in Chicago. When I was approached about joining a gang, my answer was an unequivocal no! (It was that or face the wrath of my parents). I would rather have run through fire with gasoline-soaked underwear than even think about being a part of any gang.

One day on the playground, I was surrounded by six other students, telling me that I was going to be a member of their gang or I was going to get beat up. (**Side Note 5:** My mindset was that if you were a threat to me, I was going to make sure you were never going to threaten me again by being fierce and ruthless.) When all was said and done, I was the only one left standing. In today's world, I probably would have been shot and

Life in Chicago

killed later, but back then, we still settled fights with our fists. I was afraid, so I left school and ran home. I got a spanking for fighting at school, but after that, the gangs left me alone.

The next incident I got into trouble at school for happened after a fire drill. The teacher told me to stand in front of the drinking fountain. I was told that no one could get a drink, including myself. Soon, the class bully came up to me and asked what did I think I was doing. I told him what the teacher had told me to do, and he said, "I want a drink of water," and pushed me, but I didn't budge. He then made a move like he was reaching for a weapon. I went for my back pocket and pulled out a sharp #2 pencil and stabbed him with it. When he opened up his hand, it was bloody, and blood was shooting everywhere. I left school again and ran home. A few minutes later, the principal, my teacher, and the police came to our house to question me about the incident. Needless to say, I got spanked for stabbing the boy. I didn't get any more trouble after that in Chicago.

Learned Life Lesson: Fighting is not okay. I learned that I'd better not start a fight, and if I must fight, it had better be just to defend myself and not to be a bully. Dad made it perfectly clear: "Don't start a fight, but you better not run from one, even if you get beat up. I'm not raising any sissies. Remember just because you may be larger than other kids and think that you can bully them around, don't. A scared person can become desperate and really mess you up."

As a youngster, when I got into trouble for fighting, it made me wonder—I didn't start the fight, but when I defended myself as taught, why did I get a spanking? It didn't seem fair to me, and it was never explained, but life moves on.

Back to Muncie

After we had been living in Chicago for three years, Mama Sally's health began to deteriorate back in Muncie. When there was talk about putting her into a nursing home, my mom said no, and we moved back to Muncie in 1960.

After we moved back to Muncie, I only had four more fights while growing up. The most memorable was the last one in which a girl wanted to fight me. Why she wanted to fight me I don't know, but I resisted until she found the right button to push. She hit me and uttered curse words about my mother. I snapped, turned, and hit her one time upside the head. Her eyes rolled back into her head, and she fainted. I was scared to death. I was only about eleven years old, but that taught me to never hit a girl ever again. For that incident, I got the worst spanking in my life—first from Mama and then from Dad. But during that time, you didn't say anything bad about anyone's mother. Dad could be talked about, but you dare not say anything bad about Mama!

It was about this time I learned how to hustle. I learned how to sell pop bottles, tin, brass, aluminum, lead, and copper at the scrap yard. I would also cut lawns in the spring and summer, rake leaves in the fall, and even shovel snow in the winter months to earn money. It was a wonderful feeling to earn money doing these things and be able to buy anything that I was the first person in my family to own (like a new pair of pants with no patches). A lot of what I earned went to the household, but I was allowed to keep a little for myself. I would buy some of the things that other children had like gym shoes other than PF Flyers, normal shoes instead of brogans, candy, and other small things. It was like no other feeling I'd experienced in my life at that time.

Time had progressed to the year 1964. It was a turbulent time all across the United States. The Civil Rights movement was going strong. There were marches in Muncie, and there were riots at school. I wasn't allowed to participate except to keep someone from attacking or hurting me. Also, I was allowed to participate in football and wrestling at school, and if I had been caught taking part in the riots, I would have been kicked off the teams.

Sports was my first love; I saw it as a way to better my situation in life. My most memorable time in sports was when I was on the wrestling team at 145 pounds. I had to wrestle the only guy who had beat me twice before. The first time we met, he'd injured my arm. The second time we met, I was still healing from our first match, but in the match for the city championships, I was completely healed. The match seemed to last forever. He would almost pin me; then I would almost pin him. We were going after each other like King Kong and Mighty Joe Young. I finally wore him down enough and was able to pin him. The crowd exploded with cheers because they hadn't expected me to beat the only guy who had won against me in the two previous matches. This was the first time in my life I felt like I had some worth and that I was special. This was so important to me because for most of my life, I had been told by certain members of my mom's family that I wasn't going to amount to anything and that I was going to end up like those men down on Willard and Hackley (a place where the drunks and drug pushers hung out). I was determined that I was not going to give them the satisfaction to be able to say, "I told you that you that you weren't going to amount to anything—now look at you."

(**Side Note 6:** My mother was the youngest of her six siblings. For whatever reason, my relatives were not that encouraging or helpful (that I remember) to us. It was hard for me to understand because her other siblings had good jobs or businesses, homes, etc.—good lives. Yet they were of little to no help to us. I wasn't a bad kid. I never stole anything from them, never told any lies on them, but for whatever reason, they didn't care much for me or my family.) This was also about the time that I became painfully aware of the racism in America.

It was 1968, and I was sixteen. A family friend who lived two blocks from me had a son who was in the Army who was killed only seven days in to his six-year obligation. (**Side Note 7:** It was my understanding that he should have been taken off the front lines because his time there was short, but because he was black, he wasn't.) This was hard for me because I knew him. When his body got back to Muncie, there was a big controversy because they didn't want to bury him with the other vets because he was black. You can't imagine how painful this was for me, and I wasn't even a family member. You can lose your son in the defense of America but have to fight for the right for him to be buried with the other veterans who also paid the ultimate price. Separate and unequal was still very much the norm in this country.

Learned Life Lesson - Life is hard, and it has never been fair. Through my experiences, I learned that I had worth. I also learned that the most respect I could have for anyone was to respect myself first, thus avoiding the gray areas that can lead to conflict. I also learned how to control my temper because if you don't learn self-control, you will find yourself in a position where someone else is controlling you. It's very important that you keep as much control over your life as possible.

It was about this time that I met my future wife. We were both young, but she was my bright and morning star. At the time, I often wondered what she saw in me. (She told me later.) My folks were poor, and all I had was the desire to want and be better in life. But after fifty years of marriage, six children, and fourteen grandchildren, I'm glad she chose me.

Learned Life Lesson - At a certain time in all of our lives, we will encounter certain people. We may not know what these people will bring into our lives, but there's something about their presence that just feels right. Also, sometimes other people can see your gifts that you may not see in yourself and will help you develop them, which will bring out your greatest good! That's what Phyl and her mother did for me. In the forty years I was blessed to know my mother-in-law, she always had words of encouragement for me. Whenever

Back to Muncie

I would ask her about anything, she would say, "You're smart, and I can't see any reason that you can't do that." She was a soft-spoken woman who never raised her voice at me or had a harsh word when we spoke. I wrote inspirational poetry, and she would always read my work and reply, "Son, that was beautiful. Have you ever considered publishing any of your writings? You really should!" She was my sounding board, and she is sorely missed!

About this time, my dad had an accident on his job in Chicago. A train boxcar door had fallen on him. Mom left Muncie to go to Chicago to care for Dad. He was badly injured, and the doctors told him and Mom that he would probably never be able to walk again. But my pops was stubborn, and with his Mississippi mindset, he took what the doctors told him with a grain of salt. He walked again—not as fast as he could before, but he was able to get around okay.

While Mom was in Chicago taking care of Dad, Aunt Amy, her older sister, came to Muncie to look after us for about a month. While she was there, she sent my two younger brothers and me to church. One of my brothers didn't have any shoes to wear, so she sent him to church barefoot. I felt she was totally wrong to send him to church like that, so I wouldn't let him go in. When Aunt Amy found out what I had done, she asked me why, and I told her that I felt that sending a child to church without shoes was wrong and evil. I got a spanking, but I really didn't mind because I felt I was right. I wondered later if she would have done that to her own child.

Learned Life Lesson - I learned how to be strong, even when life drops on you like a 2,000-pound train boxcar door and you're told you'll never walk again. Dad, I love how you showed me your God-given strength that led you to be able to walk after the doctors said you would not. I also learned how not to be cruel to others because that's just a foul place to come from in life.

Learned Life Lesson – You have to stand up for what you believe, even if you get in trouble.

Married Life

Phyl and I met when we were both in the tenth grade, and we were together most of that time. I think we broke up maybe once or twice. On July 19, 1969, we were married, and our first child arrived on October 3, 1969. We were both seventeen years old. She was a beautiful baby and full of life. When she was almost six months old, tragedy struck, however. On April 13, 1970, after being at work for a few hours, I got a call from my Phyl telling me that Chiondra was sick, and we needed to get her to the hospital. I arranged for us to take her there, and while we were en route to the hospital, I heard Chiondra take her last breath. I started CPR immediately, but it didn't seem to work. After arriving at the hospital, Chiondra was taken right in. After about an hour, the doctor came out and told us she had passed away. It was hard to wrap my mind around why my child had died. She had never wanted for anything, the little time that she was with us. If I got close to running out of anything Chiondra needed, I would go to my parents' house a half a block away and get money from them and go get it. After the autopsy, it was discovered that she had had spinal meningitis. After her funeral service, it was hard to get back to some sense of normalcy. Phyl was depressed for a long time. But we were able to make it through, and I thanked God through this troubled time.

Learned Life Lesson - Life is short, but it is also sweet. Live life to the fullest and be kind to all you meet. Even through tribulation, stick with God and know that He will see you through. Let the victory be God's, and as a benefit to you, the problem will be taken care of, and He will continue to guide you and protect you. No parents should have to bury their child. True prosperity is for your children to outlive you and do better for their children than you were able to do for them!

Military Life

Being young and without high school diplomas was very rough for Phyl and me. I had odd jobs, but finding a permanent job was difficult, and we had just lost our daughter. I was 18 and a half years old when I received my invitation to the draft at the time the Vietnam War was raging. Because of the earlier experience with the Williams' family, I was absolutely determined I wasn't going into the Army. So, on November 10, 1970, I joined the U.S. Navy. (I didn't realize I should have notified the Army that I joined the Navy. When I was at NAS Pensacola, the regular police and the military police came to my parents' house to arrest me because they thought I was dodging the draft.) Since I was already in the military, all was well.

Basic training in Great Lakes, Illinois, was extremely cold. As I was getting close to finishing the twelve weeks of basic training, I caught pneumonia and had a high temperature. The base doctor put me on bedrest for three days. I went back to the barracks and got into bed. The rest of our company was getting ready for an inspection. I was the master of arms for my unit, but since I was sick, my alternate took my place. I don't know why, but he decided to try to make me get out of bed to help clean the barracks. I told him I was sick and that I had a slip from the doctor for three days of bedrest. We exchanged some words, and I asked him if he had MD behind his name. This made him angry. Then he said, "Nigger, I said," and snatched me out of my bunk. When it was all over, he had a concussion, broken jaw, broken collar bone, and three cracked ribs. Thankfully, there were sixty other sailors who saw what happened, and they pulled me off of him. I was threatened with a court martial until they found out that what I had told them about the incident was true! He had attacked me, and I was just defending myself. After the incident, my drill instructor told me that if this was the old Navy, he would have taken me somewhere private and beaten me up. They moved him to another company because they didn't want us to run into each other again. (**Navy Note to file:** If attacked, he will defend himself.)

After boot camp, I was sent to Millington, Tennessee, for a month of fleet training. To my utter amazement, I found out that they had riot patrol watches on a government installation. I had only been there for a month, and there were two race riots on base! Since different places were trouble spots, one place I learned to avoid was the enlisted men's club. Too many fights broke out, and I wasn't interested in participating, willing or otherwise. Drunk men seemed to always want to fight on and off base.

Another incident that happened to me was when I was going roller skating off the base in Memphis, Tennessee. While I was standing alone at a bus stop, I saw three white sailors on the opposite side of the street. As they got closer, I could hear them saying, "We got us a nigger by himself. Let's kick his black ass." I had my pair of skates (size 12) slung around my shoulders, and when I was finished defending myself, they were lying on the ground. The bus came, I got on, and I went to the skating rink.

After I finished my training at Millington, Tennessee, I was transferred to Naval Air Station in Pensacola, Florida, a training station for pilots. It was a constant, daily fight for the eleven months I was there to get medical treatment. I had weeping eczema, a skin condition that broke out in all the moist folds of my body. I was assigned to the wash rack area, where I washed aircraft. The soap we used caused my eczema to flare up, and the heat of Florida made my condition even worse. The weeping eczema produced a fluid that made my skin and any scabs I had stick to my uniform. It also made me want to scratch the areas, which made the problem worse. After seeing a dermatologist for the third time, I requested to be considered for a medical discharge, and the doctor said no. I really don't know what oaths doctors take when caring for people, but the doctors I came into contact with on base were hostile and less

Military Life

than helpful. He refused to give me any medication for my eczema. It took contacting the Red Cross and my congressman for me to get treatment. When I saw him again, he was very upset, but he treated my eczema and removed me off the wash rack. He threatened me, saying, "You can get into a lot of trouble about what you write home about." I became the nigger that didn't know my place. I went to the legal department to see if the officer could be brought up on charges. Within a month, I was transferred from NAS, Pensacola, Florida, to the USS *Hancock* (CVA-19 – "the Hacking Hanna") to Vietnam. (I was supposed to be in Florida for two years, but the white officers decided I needed to go.)

When I arrived on the USS *Hancock*, I was assigned to the mess cooking department, which for me meant carrying 200-300 pounds of frozen food strapped to my back from the freezers to the mess deck to be cooked. This was what I did 8-10 hours a day for the first three months that I was on the ship. After that, I did three months of compartment cleaning, which consisted of mopping, sweeping, and dusting to make sure everything was white-glove clean.

My next job on the ship was in the ground support section as a maintenance administration man, which meant taking care of logging and scheduling maintenance for the ground support equipment aboard the aircraft carrier. This was an interesting shop to be in (not in a good way). I was the only black man in this shop, and most of the white sailors were extremely hostile and very racist. I kept to myself. When I would leave and come back, if there were conversations going on, everyone would go quiet when I walked in. Also, the ridiculous and assumed ideas about black people were just mind-blowing. They seemed to be amazed that not only did I do my job well but I was able to communicate well. On one annual review, one of the comments was that "I had very good command of the English language, both oral and written." The review was good, but really? It was as if they thought I was a trained gorilla. I just shut out the racism and did what I had to do to keep calm and do my job.

Military Life

Because I didn't fit with their idea of how I should be, it seemed as some of them hated me more...almost as if I had showed up their racist beliefs and exposed them as bigots. This was my life for two years—watching my back from attacks from hostile whites (enlisted men as well as officers) to keep them from railroading me into an incident that would get me sent to the brig (jail) or get a bad conduct or dishonorable discharge. I saw at least five or six black sailors in my division alone get sent to the brig. When they got out, they were sent back to the same area and had to work in an even more hostile environment. They were literally in a double jeopardy situation—they couldn't go to a better environment, and if they "didn't act right" according to their tormentors, their lives would be ruined with an undesirable discharge. With God's help, thankfully, I was able to navigate around all this stuff. The only relief I had from the constant atmosphere of hostility was when I was "safely" back in my quarters with the other black sailors.

The day came when it was time for me to leave the military. On my last day in the Navy, I had a problem with the payroll office. The officer didn't want to pay me for my fifty-nine days of leave that I had on the books. Plus, he talked to me like I was some sort of animal. I went to my department's head of office and explained the problem I was having with payroll and asked if he would call down to payroll and tell them to pay me so that I could leave. The commander was upset about what I had told him (there were some good officers) and said, "Sure, David." I went back down to payroll, and the officer was very upset with me and told me, "I was going to pay your black ass." Then I asked him if he wanted me to go back to my department's head of office to tell him what he had just said to me. That was my sendoff from the Navy back to civilian life—no, "Thank you for your service," or, "Good luck in civilian life;" nothing.

(**Side Note 8:** When I went into the Navy, it was my intention to make a career in the military. When I got in and saw the rampant racism and that there was very little justice, I knew I wouldn't be able to last long in that environment. If a white sailor did something wrong and a black man of superior rank wrote

Military Life

him up, often the black person was demoted in rank for daring to write up a white man. That career path was closed for me.)

(**Side Note 9:** Before I got out of the Navy, I was given the GAF—Global Assessment Function test. The GAF score determines how well a person will adjust going from military life to civilian life. Scoring is from 0 to 100 points. The closer to 100 you are shows you have a better chance of success in civilian life. Anywhere between zero and 30 was supposed to be mean a very difficult time, and 31-40 was not that good. When I was discharged, my GAF score was 35. With a lower GAF, you were supposed to receive assistance upon getting out to help you become ready for the civilian world. I didn't know at the time that I was eligible for services, and no one told me. I was released back into the civilian world without any help or training to make my transition easier.)

Back to Civilian Life

Adjusting back to civilian life was not easy. One moment I was in a war zone with planes taking off and landing, bombs going off in the distance, and ship and crew on alert for a possible attack. Then the next moment, I was back at home—no loud aircraft, no dodging of enemy ships, etc. I was able to drink and bathe in clean water not poisoned by chemicals and was able to eat food that hadn't been prepared with contaminated water (that had been filtered and cleaned) and was properly cooked and delicious. I didn't have to watch my back or worry about getting trapped in bad situations by whites, and I was away from the constant, unrelenting hostile environment. This was all good, but I had changed drastically.

I was hyper anxious about people being behind me or being in a crowd. When I went somewhere, I walked the area carefully to find out how to get out quickly. I still dreamed about being attacked, and I would wake up fighting. I was jittery and suspicious when I heard a car backfire or some other loud, sudden noise (at least once, I ducked behind a car when Phyl and I were walking). I had and continue to have periods of black, black moods of depression. It's as if a black cloud comes down, and I can only see everything through a darkened lens.

People couldn't walk up to me quickly. I would go into a fighting stance before I could stop myself. I had to be extremely careful around the children and Phyl because I was always on the alert for anything that seemed to be a threat, and several times, I lashed out when surprised. I won't go into all the mental and physical changes I experienced and that Phyl noticed, but suffice it to say, I wasn't the same person that she'd married before going into the service.

When I got out of the service, I was hired through the Veteran's Readjustment Act and was able to get a job at NAS Alameda. (At the time, I didn't know it, but there was a saying that NAS Alameda was for white people, and the Naval Supply Center Oakland was for black people.) It took a month to get my security clearance (even though I had had security clearance in the Navy, but this is what I was told). I was hired as a GS3, making $3.25 an hour. (I found out years later that as a veteran, I should have started out as a WG5, making $5.25 an hour, but that information wasn't given to me, and I didn't know to ask.) It took me almost two years to get to WG5). Since we were expecting our third child, that wasn't enough money, so I decided to go to junior college. At that time, the cost to do so was small. The money I got paid for going to school supplemented my low-paying job.

After a few years of working and going to school, it was finally time for me to graduate from college. My mother and my baby brother came out from Muncie to see me get my associate's degree. I was the second child in my family to even attempt going to college and was so proud because I had done this while having a large family of my own. My mother told me, "Son, I'm so proud of you and Phyl and these lovely grandbabies (we had four children at the time). They are well-mannered and very well-taken care of. You guys have done a wonderful job of raising these children." Phyl and I felt very proud because there is no greater feeling than to have your parents tell you how good a job you've done at being a parent.

I was always looking to advance at work, so my next step was to get into the apprenticeship program on base. I took the test, passed it with a high score, went to the interview, and took my test scores to show that I had maintained a 3.5 GPA (I was a senior at San Francisco State), and it still took me took me six years to get into the program. Later, in reading the base paper, I realized that the people who were accepted quickly were mostly white women who may have handed someone a screwdriver (a slight exaggeration, but not by much). I had way more work experience and more education than many of the people who were listed and highlighted in the base paper. I realized it took me so long to get into the program because I was a black man.

I finally graduated from the apprenticeship program. I was now a certified aircraft sheet metal mechanic with Department of Defense certification. Being a mechanic offered me a career that would take me around the world fixing aircraft.

The other part of being a mechanic was to train new apprentices. I wasn't allowed to advance, and often, the apprentices I trained would become my boss with way less experience and several without the work ethic to do the job. I would apply for higher jobs, but I was never promoted above an aircraft sheet metal mechanic, and I was limited to working on certain aircraft. The newer aircraft required more specialized training, and the people in charge made sure it was the "right" people who were trained and able to work on those aircraft.

I could go on about the times when unqualified supervisors had to be taught how to read a schematic to approve the completed work to "pass" the quality test or the times when people would intentionally work at half-speed until overtime was needed to get the jobs done and then almost work at regular speed to keep the overtime going for a while. I didn't have time for the games. I went to work to get my job done and to do it well. I made them look bad, so there was resentment toward me.

Over the years, the people in charge became so ridiculously racist, firing people unlawfully, writing people up for stupid stuff, and purposely setting traps to have a reason to fire people. It was like being back in the military. Finally, it got so bad that the black employees had to sue the base to make those in charge act right. During the trial, supervisors claimed they couldn't collaborate some of my details because I had "lost" my personnel file. (What employee at that time had control of his or her personnel file?) Unfortunately for them, I had kept an extensive, daily journal, and it was clear to the court that the base was in the wrong. I won my case. The other people who had been wrongfully terminated were rehired and able to get their jobs back with back pay. Still, with all the job craziness, I had a good career,

Back to Civilian Life

and it enabled me to provide well for my family, and for that, I am thankful.

I'm going to end my book here. We had a lot of trials and tribulations as all families do (teen challenges—we had five teens at one time—marriage challenges, job challenges, etc., just normal and some not-so-normal challenges of life), but Phyl and I went on to earn a six-figure income, buy homes and cars, and give our children a better life then we had when we were growing up. It took a lot of work, but both of us were up to the challenge.

Last Thoughts and Ending Prayers

I will end my story with a prayer. I pray that the next phase of your journey will be the biggest blessing to you. First, you need to develop a relationship with God because He will be with you even when your brother, sister, mom, and dad turn their backs on you. Looking at your life, I pray that you will see how the trials you experienced were lessons of life that you needed to learn because when you don't learn from your mistakes in life, you'll most often repeat them, and they may cost you more than they did before. Every trial and tribulation you've faced in your life was a learning experience for you to learn from and to help bring out the very best of the good that God has placed in each and every one of us.

Unless you are an actor or very good in sports or music, your talents may not be obvious, but know that 1 Corinthians 7:7 says, "I wish that all men were as I am, but each man has his own gift from God; one has this gift and another has that." We all have different gifts from God. Discover what those gifts are and use them for God's glory, and watch how much better your life will become.

Also, thank God for all those in your life who were mean or abusive towards you. It will help you to be a far greater person than those who did you harm. Also, forgive them for what they did to you. When you do this, you take your power back and the control they had over you, and you won't become a bitter person. No one wants to be around bitter people. I know that if you have courage enough to give God a try, the change in your life will be so great it will literally make you cry. Only a fool will continue to do the same thing and expect different results. My dad used to say, "A wise man does first what a fool does last."

Last Thoughts and Ending Prayers

Dear God, I want to thank you for all the blessings that You have bestowed on me. You've given me a loving wife and family along with long life as well as wisdom for these sixty-eight years of my life. The wife You blessed me with and our fourteen grandchildren have been the driving force behind me. I also thank you for these words of encouragement and for all who will read as they come along after us. Proverbs 20:29 says, "The glory of a young man is their strength and the splendor of old man is their gray head."

Bless the generations that come behind me to be the blessing that You intend for them. Help them to see Psalm 37:25, "I have been young and now I am old; yet I have not seen the righteous forsaken, nor their descendants begging broad."

Lord, I pray that You show the youngsters that they have to become teachers to show those younger than themselves the importance of having a relationship with You and about trying to do the right things in life, as well as the importance of each and every person's life and the lessons that can be learned.

To readers, this is the reason I wrote this book. You should consider your story and know that writing about your experiences could provide hope to some young man or young woman who after reading about your story will make the wiser choice for his or her life. Every person's story, though different, will have similarities that will benefit someone else. I may never know if my psalm (story) will help anyone else, but if it helps one person not to be caught up by the traps and snares of this society, it will have been time well spent, and to God be the glory!

You have no idea the greatness that God has blessed each and every one of us with, and like talents, gifts, and love, these are of little use unless they are shared. Your psalm is about your experiences—your life story, if you will—that when shared will be a mighty blessing for some young person and could prevent him or her from spending a lifetime in jail or an eternity in hell. I pray that these words of encouragement end up being a blessing for you as much as the joy it was for me to share the story of my life. I thank God for this and pray

Last Thoughts and Ending Prayers

that this will bless all humanity. I've included some of my poetry so you can see how something as beautiful as these poems could have come from someone like me.

One Love

Writing Poetry

When I was an active member of Faith Presbyterian Church in Oakland, my church family realized that I wrote poetry, and if there was a special event, they would ask me to write a poem to be read to the congregation.

When my friends realized that I wrote poetry, they would ask me to write poems for their loved ones and the special occasions in their lives.

When significant events happened in my life, such as my thirty-third wedding anniversary, the passing of someone close, birthdays, etc., a poem would come to mind that would fit the occasion.

Here are a few poems in the following pages for you to read.

I hope you enjoy them.

One Love

Mothers' Day

This is for all the mothers and mothers-to-be.
I often wonder if you see what I see?
And it doesn't matter what your age may be
because I've seen the same traits around the world, you see!
I see maturity, compassion, encouragement, and unconditional love,
which we all know came from God through our parents to me and now you;
so when our children have children,
they will know exactly what it is
that they need to do.
Dear Lord, I thank you for the village of mothers
that I was blessed to see, and I pray that You continue
to make mothers who love You and show
their daughters
how to grow in splendor and grace throughout eternity.

One Love

Psalms in the Key of Life

Memorial Day

Dear Lord, I pray that we never forget our great debt
that we will never be able to repay to
America's brave young men and women
who gave their very best and
now have been laid to rest—
that we do all we can do to make America
the best place in the world known to me and to you.
There is nothing more humbling
than going by any national cemetery and looking
at all the white headstones,
thinking of how much I've been blessed.
And for the rest of my life,
I need to do my very best to honor those
who gave their all until there was nothing left.
Because, you see—I look and think of how easily
one of those headstones could represent me,
a Vietnam veteran.

One Love

In Time

There are times in every young man and woman's life
when our country will call upon us to go
halfway around the world to fight.
Having been taught to believe in God
and country, we respond to the call.
And for a great number of us, we gave our all.
But for those of us
who have been blessed
not to fall,
we find ourselves faced with the greatest challenge of all—
having to prove exposure to chemical elements
that the government has always had knowledge existed.
And this too-oftentimes happens
just so you can be treated,
not to mention the fact that benefits
will often be denied due to non-verifiable records.
Because you see, there are a great number of veterans

Psalms in the Key of Life

walking around
in quiet desperation.
And may God bless those affected and
forbid a repeat of the tragedy that
happened at Fort Hood, Texas,
and focus more attention on those
of us who answered the call to serve.
And in time and with the same fervor
that this government called us to serve,
they will treat and give us vets
the benefits

we

so

justly

deserve.

One Love,
David D.
Vietnam veteran

Tribute to Dr. King-

By: David L. Dollison, Sr.
1/24/2010

We all know the legacy of Rev. Dr. Martin Luther King Jr.
Please take a journey with me so that
we can see what we can get from Dr. King's legacy.

1. Dr. King was a man of God.
2. Dr. King believed in non-violence.
3. Dr. King believed in a quality education for everyone.
4. Dr. King believed in good jobs for everyone.
5. Dr. King believed in allowing everyone to develop to their full potential.

I don't know about you,
but for me, this is a road map of how blessed your life can be.
For you to be able to see,

let's look at how far God has brought me.

I came from being dirt poor in Muncie, Indiana.
Blessed to grow up and live through Vietnam,
I got a job after the service as a journeyman
aircraft sheet metal mechanic.
I have been blessed with a wife of forty and a half years,
six children, and fourteen grandchildren.
I currently own my own business working as a
janitor/security and do well with it.
I am loved by my family, co-workers, and church.
I am not famous, but I am known for the work of
my hands and my ability to write encouraging words
for family
and friends, and on top of all that, I cook some pretty
good barbeque!

I tell you this, and I know that it's true—
if God can perform such a work as me,
what will He do for you if only you ask Him to?
If Dr. King were able to ask you, "What is your dream?"

what would your answer be? Once again, my faith family, I thank God that He blessed me with these encouraging words
and pray that they uplift you in the life that God inspires you to do.

>Amen,
>One Love

Chosen

May I first say how proud I am of the choice
you've made to take a closer walk with God.
And know that even in trials and tribulations,
God will never leave or forsake you.
And even though life may have seemed to give you
the feeling
of being overlooked, left out, and passed over,
know that you have been chosen by God.
Delight yourself in Him, and He will give you the
desires of your heart,
and you will prosper in all that you do
and succeed wherever you go.
And you will be His light that
He will be able to put in any dark place
and still be an example of His love, mercy, and grace.
Because God has chosen you,
you'll be blessed, and He will make you great.
My prayer for you is that, "all mercy
and love that I have received,

Writing Poetry

you'll get ten times that amount,
and in you, may God always be pleased."

One Love
Your brother in Christ,
David L. Dollison Sr.

Psalms in the Key of Life

WHERE'S MY MAN?

We can be so critical of ourselves sometimes
that we are unable to see the goodness that we have,
that the rest of the world can see.
If you allow me,
I'd like to say some of your qualities that I notice most
every day.
You have a wonderful personality that is truly great.
You carry yourself with splendor and grace,
and, girl, that smile of yours could
light up the world.
Trust God to provide for the emptiness that
you may feel.
And when He does, your relationship will be lasting
and oh-so-very real.
You've trusted God when your life seemed so unreal;
trust Him again,
and He will surely see you through.
I'm sure that with the love that you have
and the need to share that love,

Writing Poetry

God will send you the man who will be good
enough for you
and will be a total asset and a joy
that is deserving of the wonderful person that is you.

One Love

33 Years

Taking time to reflect over these precious years, the life we've had is enough to bring one cheer. I often wonder just where I would be without you and you without me. And then it comes to mind that nothing in life is unless God wants it to be! I also know that this isn't all that God has for you and me. I look forward to seeing where we will be because it's
obvious it's supposed to be you and me. I don't know where we're going down this road of life, but when we get there, I'm sure we'll still be husband and wife. I hope the words bring as much joy to you as they did for me, so there is nothing more for me to
say but **happy anniversary!**

David L. Dollison Sr.

SECRETS

Secrets are the things that we want to stay hidden.
It would surprise and even shock the ones
closest to us
if it were to become known what we've done.
It causes a wall of lies and mistrust,
and you hope and pray that the dam never busts.
So, to avoid the problems that secrets usually bring,
be truthful as possible by all means and in all things.

One Love

Psalms in the Key of Life

A Good Man

Who's to say what a good man is to be;
here's what the term did for me.
It gave me a strong love for God and my family.
It gave me the strength to stop using alcohol
and drugs.
It gave me the strength to replace anger with love.
I'd like to apologize for not measuring up
to what you thought of me.
But you should be thankful to God
that I'm not the person I used to be.
For those in my life who I've let down,
I'm grateful to God He put my feet on more
solid ground.
So, when life seems like you've fallen into a pit, lift
your head to heaven and remember this—
with God's mercy and unconditional love,
He will change your situation for the good
that the human mind can conceive of.

Writing Poetry

When you've done all the wrong in life that you think you can,
look to God because He can make us all good men.

Legacy

Have you ever given thought to what your
legacy might be?
And whatever your preference may be, there are many
women of color for you young ladies
and many men of color for our young men who are
wonderful examples of what you can turn out to be.
Because if you look back in history,
I'm sure that you'll see some young brother
or young sister
who got the right encouragement from an
older person
who helped them be all that they could be.
When you learn from your history,
you can create a better future.
We all are here on this earth because we are special
with the talent and skills that God has blessed us with.
And if you're not sure what those talents and skills are,
ask God, and He will make it clear. Then use that
skill for God,

Writing Poetry

and He will bless you and make you great.
And in time, you'll go from this place
to being known by a large portion of the human race.
I really look forward to seeing how many of our
young and beautiful sisters and brothers
grow up and do many good things that will
make this world a better place.
And your legacy will be great.

One Love

Psalms in the Key of Life

THE MAKING OF A BLACK MAN

I am the man who stood proud from the moment of
your birth ---
who gave all I had even when it hurt;
who with God's help, I was able to show you the
things in life that work.
God helped me to show you right from wrong
and, most importantly, how to be strong.
My prayer is
I hope these lessons work better for you ---
when you become me ---
and continue to work for you long after I'm
just a memory.

Your loving father,
David D.
One Love

CARE TO LOVE

I'd like to tell you about a man, Mr. Gene Langille—
a man who cared about everyone,
especially those who came into his circle of life.
Some people have a circle large enough for them and
their family;
Gene, on the other hand, had a circle big enough that
there was room for you too!
A man diverse enough in his thinking to be an
encourager for everyone with hope and a dream; A
man who on our first face-to face meeting left me
alone in their new home for four hours
while he and my wife went shopping,
which was so special to me.

A man who told me that he was so grateful for the
diverseness in his life
because it made me a better person and greatly
improved my life.

Psalms in the Key of Life

Mr. Langille, in tribute for being a good example of
a husband,
father, teacher, and a dear and trusted friend,
for caring until that care turned to love,
I thank God for this learned life lesson that
can take anyone from caring to love.
Dear God, I thank you for the blessing and
encouragement
you gave me through Gene Langille
to continue to write supportive and
encouraging words such as these.

Your child in Jesus Christ,
David L. Dollison Sr.

Chains

Chains are made to bind things together to keep
them from falling apart.
But no number of chains can bind one's mind or heart.
Those words came to me when I received your letter,
and the Saul who I grew up with is so much stronger
than that!
If you have any doubts about your ability to do this,
ask God to give you the strength and the wisdom
to overcome.
Because God can make a way when there seems to be
no way that is humanly possible.
Don't take my word for this.
I'm sure there are people who you talk to and value
their advice;
ask them and see what they tell you!
Anytime in life you get the same advice from two or
more people
who you know haven't talked to each other,
it's something that you might want to pay attention to.

Psalms in the Key of Life

Philippians 1:6—"Being confident of this very thing, the he (God) which hath begun a good work in you will perform it until the day of Jesus Christ. If ever you feel like you, don't think you are going to make it, read this and may it give you the strength you need so that you do."

I love you!
Your brother,
David.

Writing Poetry

HAPPY 55TH

My Dear Brother,

First, I'd like to say happy 55th birthday to you!
Please accept my humble poem that I pray will brighten this day too.
I want to say thank you for all that you do because some of the things you've done,
I was unable to.
And as I write this, I'm thinking about how wonderful God is to have blessed me with a brother as wonderful as you! (smile)
The way you looked after Mama and Daddy until God called them home;
The way you became mediator to our nieces and nephews when our younger brothers got sent to prison
and how much they love and respect you.

So, you see that this poem's time was due;

they don't make birthday cards that are worthy to celebrate the love that is you.
God, in His wisdom and grace,
through Mama and Daddy put such a large heart in you that makes it possible for you to positively affect everyone who comes in contact with you.

With all the love and respect that this, your day, should bring,
my prayer is that every time you read this poem, your heart will sing.

>One Love
>Your brother,
>David

To Marcus, My Son

The first thing I'd like to say is,
"I love you, and you mean so much to me."
And now, the time has come in your life
where no restraining order and no more lies
can ever come between us for the rest of my life.
You know the struggle I had trying to be a father to you.
But I can only imagine how difficult it was for a young man like you.
But thank God, you, my son, persevere, and for that I love you.
I need you to know that if you have a need or you just want to talk to me,
any time day or night, believe me, my son, you've earned that right.
Marcus, I need for you to do a few things for me.
I need you to keep your focus and to stay on track.
Marcus, I need you to persevere again
and finish this race by completing your studies and
get your Bachelor of Science Degree in Sociology

from UC Santa Cruz.
And don't let anything but death
keep you from accomplishing this worthwhile goal.
I have some learned life lessons
I'd like for you to give some thought to
to be a self-assured man but also to be humble.
Be a man who is calm in the storm and don't be defensive.
Respect people at all levels in life
because, son, titles don't inspire or influence people,
but your actions most certainly will. Revere God and your elders (history),
and He will ensure your future.
I know this may seem very heavy,
but I've just written to my son about
what will bring you the greatest pleasure and success
in your life.
My prayer is that your success will be so great
 that you will pass it on to your family, whenever that takes place.
I offer this little bit of wisdom because I love you.
And if you are wise enough and follow through,

Writing Poetry

you'll be amazed at how good life will be for you.
Son, wisdom that is not passed on is soon lost!
I've written you these things because they are true,
and my love for you is that great too.
You'll become a leader of many
and will be a positive influence in a lot of people's lives
and be our joy for the rest of your mother and father's
natural lives.

One Love, your loving father

Mama's Girl

It's a beautiful sight to see the shared love between a mother and her little girl. Mom will show her how to navigate in this world, which most oftentimes is extremely hard for Mama's girl. Mama will show you how to deal with the challenges of life and to do it with splendor and grace. Because Mama knows how quickly time passes, and before long, Mama's girl will be taking her place, showing their little girl how best she can deal with the human race.

Writing Poetry

BE YOUNG, BE FOOLISH, BUT BE HAPPY

We all have been young, and in being young,
we all have
a tendency of doing some pretty foolish things.
And as God blesses us with time and wisdom,
most of us will put the foolish things of life behind us.
And the more we grow in God's wisdom and grace,
we'll be blessed with a happiness that this
mean world from us cannot take.
This world can't understand the peace that they can
see in your face,
when life around you seems so mixed up and so
out of place.
Something to consider. Lord, if I don't have
the sense or
the strength to hold onto Your hand, please don't let
go of mine.
Thanks for guiding me through my youth and from
being a fool

Psalms in the Key of Life

to becoming a wise man, and I pray that You'll be my
happiness for as long as
I live in this land and for all mankind.

One Love: David L. Dollison

Writing Poetry

A CELEBRATION OF LIFE – REVEREND DOCTOR FRANK JACKSON

Glory to God for Your love, wisdom, and grace
and for blessing us with your servant
the Reverend Doctor Frank Jackson to guide us while
we're in this place.
Pastor Jackson was more, much more, than our pastor.
He was an advisor, counselor, and dear friend.
When the world around us seemed to be crumbling down,
Pastor Jackson would use God's Word
to put our feet back on solid ground.
Pastor Jackson would also use encouraging words
to lift you up when having done all you can,
you thought you had reached your end.
Pastor Jackson would smile and say, "Let God begin!"
Know this, my faith family—there are no chance
meetings in life.
God in His wisdom will put people like Pastor
Jackson into your life

Psalms in the Key of Life

who you will listen to,
who will make a major difference in your life.
God, through Pastor Jackson, made me a better father
to my children,
grandfather to my children's children,
and husband to my wife,
Pastor Jackson has brought me closer seeking our
Lord and Savior Jesus Christ.
What a legacy and a blessing to have been in touch
with the likes of a Pastor Jackson
and his faith family.
Dear Lord, thanks for blessing us with
the Reverend Doctor Frank Jackson,
and we pray that You keep his spirit until we
all come together again in heaven.
And let all God's people say Amen.

One Love,
David L. Dollison, Sr.

GRANDSON

Now that you've had some time for reflection,
please allow me to point out what I hope
you've learned
from this "learned life lesson."
First, you should know that God loves you
a thousand times more than the people you
consider family are able to do.
We adults are not the enemy
because we have seen the traps and snares
that are set up to make you a part of the prison
system or dead.
I'm giving you a book that you should read along with
the Bible.
If you ask God to come into your life and help you
to do right,
you'll be surprised by the changes He will make.
And as a result of the change, how much of a blessing
you'll be in other young people's lives.
There is no place God can't go!

Psalms in the Key of Life

There is no person God cannot save!
There is no power that God cannot overcome.
And there is no person He saves that
He will not use to save someone else!
Son, I write this to you to let you know that
I love you, and God does too.
Keep your chin up and know that God will see
you through
this trail and the rest of your life.
One Love, Papa D.

JASON

Having come from a humble beginning, you know from experience how it feels when someone you know and love is facing their ending.
But from being a miracle yourself, it's your time to be that miracle for someone else.
For having a heart as large as you do,
you are the only person who can be the comforter for your nephew.
God knows that your heart is heavy, and believe me, my brother, He will fix that too for you.
Just like you trusted God and were prayed over
when you were in your diabetic coma,
I ask you to trust and believe in God to do the very same for your nephew that He did for you. Jason, I think you know that I love you too, and I pray to God that this short poem will be some comfort to you.
Also know that all of you will be in my prayers that
He will heal all His children because He cares. Your brother in Christ.

One Love:
David L. Dollison Sr.

Mona

First, I want you to know that God loves you.
He loves you so much that He's blessed you with
Little Jack too.
Remember when I asked you, "See how
blessed you are?"
You see, Mona, life without you would be like smothering one of God's stars.
So, if you're ever feeling down or low, read this poem,
and you will know that you are special and loved by a
lot of people
who want to see you grow like your Uncle
Dee and Red Pop, who will be looking down and
loving you when you reach the top.

Love you, Red Pop
David L. Dollison Sr.

THANKSGIVING

First, let's give God the glory for His love, His mercy, and His grace.
I was given the theme of Thanksgiving, which is a public celebration of divine goodness.
Here are just a few of the things that I'm thankful for.
We are alive, we've been saved by grace, we've been kept by the Lord's power divine.
These are three blessing that we all have, even if we don't have a dime in our pockets!
We are all thankful for reasonably good health, for food, and for shelter.
We are thankful because of 1 Corinthians 1:24, "But unto them which are called, both Jews, and Greeks, Christ the power of God, and the wisdom of God."
It's good to know that by seeking God and His kingdom, He will bless you with power and wisdom. Philippians 1:6: "Being confident of this very thing, that he who has begun a good work in you will complete it until the of Jesus Christ."

Psalms in the Key of Life

I don't know about you, but I'm truly thankful for this.
And even in the face of adversity, we should be thankful because
in 1 Thessalonians 5:18, it says, "In ever thing give thanks, for this is the will of God in Christ Jesus concerning you."
So, even when trouble comes into your life,
God has a plan for He said that He would never leave nor forsake us.
These are some of the things that are worthy of our praise and thanksgiving.
And let all of God's people say, Amen.

One Love
David L. Dollison Sr.

This House

I have this poem here as a constant reminder to me
of how wonderful God's love and His blessing have
been to me.
Lord, bless this house to be a place of love,
absent of confusion, malice, and anything else that is
not of Your love.
And for the grace and love that You've instilled in me,
I pray that everyone will experience this every time
they come to this house to visit me.

One Love

A Tribute to Ms. Vivian Dickens

This is my humble way of saying
thanks to a remarkable woman who graced my life.
It takes a special person who can add value to
someone else's life.
I will always remember you referring to Robert and
me as "my boys,"
knowing that this expression of love toward us was
really a joy.
As I have told my children, "When a lady claims you
as her child
and she did not give you birth,
it speaks volumes about her love for you and greatly
increases your worth."
Dear Mama, to give your love as freely as you do,
I can understand why our heavenly Father has
sent for you.
There's only one more thing that I need to
say—thank God
He allowed you to pass through my life this way,

Writing Poetry

and I hope I will have half of the effect in a positive way in someone else's life, I pray.
Have a blessed homegoing day.

Love,
David L. Dollison Sr.

Psalms in the Key of Life

Homegoing

First, I want to thank God for blessing us with
sixty-five years of Stanley Leroy Dollison,
a man who got his start from a very humble
beginning,
who lived his life giving of himself until the very end.
Some men have a circle of life
where there is only room for them.
Other men have a circle big enough for themselves
and their family,
and finally, there are men whose circle is flexible
enough that
there is room anyone to come in.
This was my beloved brother, Stanley.
He was a man who would give you the shirt
off his back
because he believed in God, and in God, there
is no lack.
God in His infinite wisdom, love, and grace

blessed you with His light that could lighten a
dark place.
This is one of those learned life lessons that if learned
and practiced,
your legacy on this earth will surely be great.
Finally, I want to tell you that you'll be amazed by the
good things in life that you can do
that are good and helpful to others,
especially when you don't expect any credit in return.
May God bless and keep you in all the things in life
that you do
and may you be a blessing in life to others as I have
tried to be to you.

One Love, Stanley L. Dollison

CPSIA information can be obtained
at www.ICGtesting.com
Printed in the USA
LVHW050934270321
682676LV00039B/2107

9 781662 810732